Grandpa
Buster
of Kitty Kingdom

Published by

Write Impression Ltd.

ISBN 978-0-473-62705-8

Copyright 2022 © Kitty Kingdom Wellington - Cat Sanctuary.

Long before this story was written,
I was a very happy little kitten.
I had a pillow and a blanket,
In my own special basket.
I could eat as much as I wanted,
And my every wish was granted.

**But then my family moved away.
I haven't seen them to this day.**

**Why they left me, I do not know.
It made me feel so sad and low.**

The new people chased me away.
For some reason,
They would not let me stay.
I no longer had a home.
I was left out on my own.

But I'm a brave cat.
I don't give up just like that.

So I wandered about for weeks,
Then months, then years.
I learned to survive,
And conquer all my fears.

I searched for a cosy place to lay my head,
But all I found was a damp, old shed.

A mouldy box in
the corner,
Did not make it
any warmer.

I'm a peaceful and friendly chap.
I do not like to fight or scrap.

But there were other lost cats too,
And there wasn't much else we could do.

We had to fight and bite
With all our might,
Just to live and eat
on that filthy street.

I was always hungry
And that dog was so angry.

When I stole a bite from his bowl,
He pounced with a savage growl.

I had nowhere to run and hide,
And so he bit me on my side.

I needed help very fast,
Or else I would not last.
I felt so sick and weak,
So helpless and meek.
I was awfully scared,
And I thought no-one cared.

But Alice came with her trap.
She lifted the flap, and put in the bait.
Then...
She stepped back to wait.

It wasn't bacon I could smell,
That I know all too well!
It was a piece of pork crackling
That I soon would be tackling.

I knew she meant well.
She was kind, I could tell.
So, Into the trap I went.
That food was heaven sent.
But then I found I couldn't get out!
I wriggled and squirmed
And twisted about.

I tore at the bars with my paws,
I pulled and tugged them with my claws.

But Alice was quiet and calm,
Even when I scratched her arm.

Then off we went in her car.
Luckily, it was not very far.

I'd never lost hope
That one day I'd find
Someone caring and loving and kind.

It was hard to give her my trust,
But I knew that to stay there I must.

Alice showed me my new room.
I didn't run, I didn't zoom.
I crept straight into my soft new bed,
Laying down my weary head.

I was painful and sore.
I could not bear it any more.
I do not fuss or ask for much,
But still I would not let her touch.

So, she rang up the vet
Who said he could not see me yet.
Alice did not like the way I looked,
Even though they were fully booked.
She knew it was an emergency.
Someone really had to help me!

My life was almost spent,
So up to the Gorge* we went.

* Wellington After Hours Veterinary Clinic

They gave me a jab,
Which made me feel fab!
Soon I was snoring,
Till the next morning!
While I slept,
They stitched me up all around.
Then, off they crept,
Leaving my wounds tightly bound.

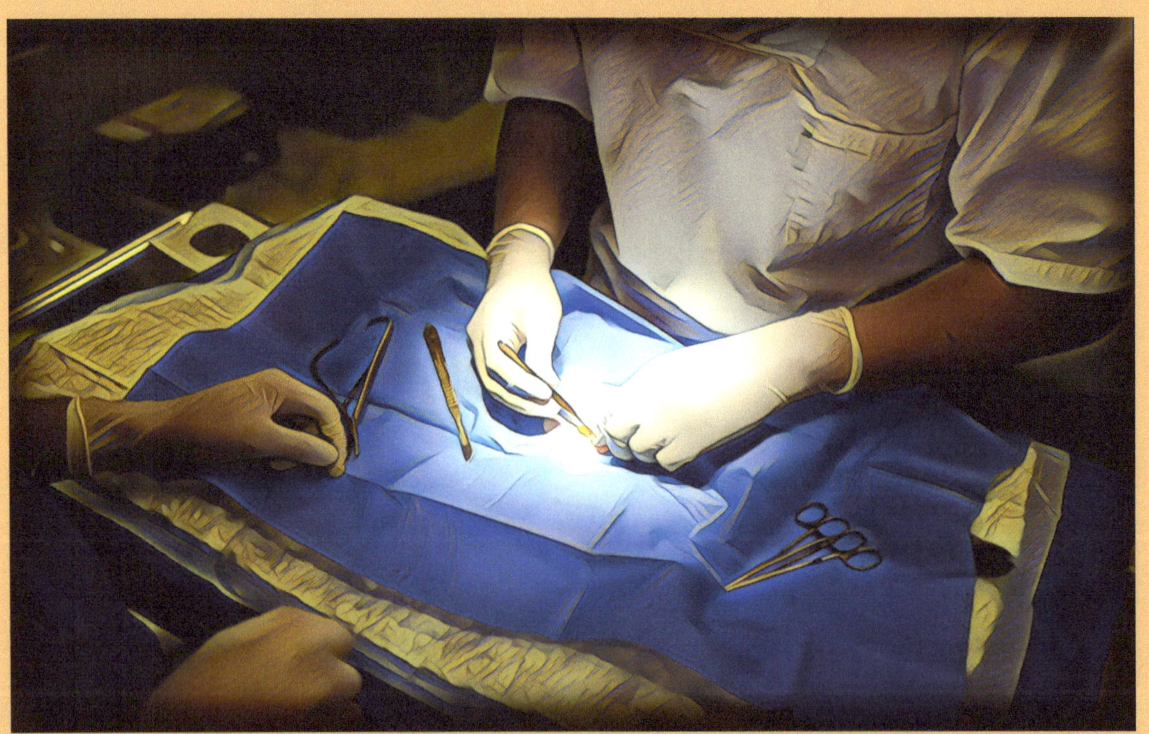

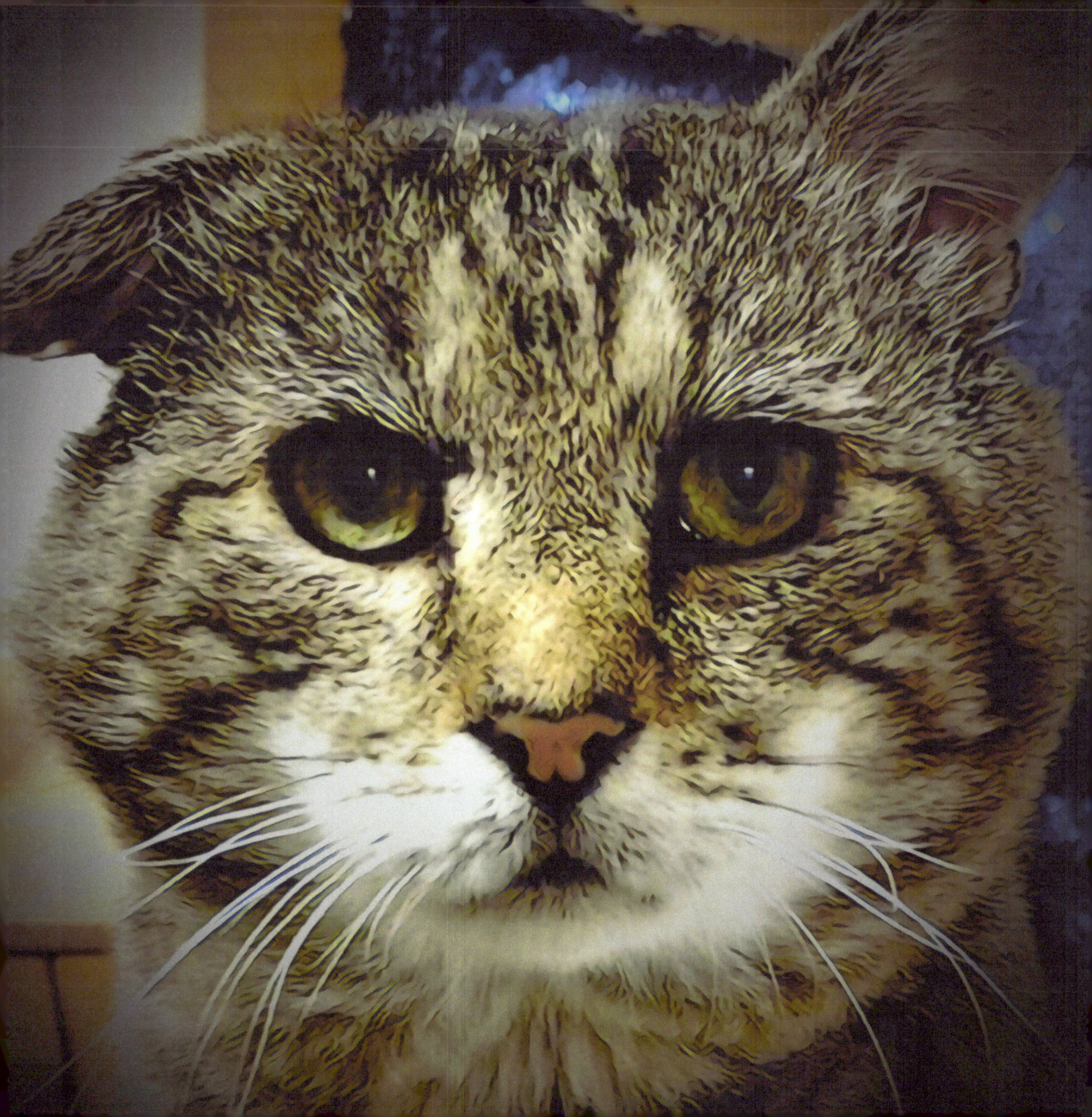

I'm a very brave cat.
There's no doubt about that!

My teeth were broken and sore,
All rotten from surface to core.
So they took them all out...
What a relief!
I felt so much better,
Beyond all belief.
I have a sore in my mouth too,
So taking my medicine is what I now do.

I was in hospital for ages,
And the account was pages and pages.
It cost so much to keep me healthy,
And as you know, I'm not very wealthy.
But kind, caring people came to my aid,
And so my bills always got paid.

My room I now had to share.
A litter of kittens had come to live there.
They were lonely and small,
But I loved them all.

It's scary for little cats on their own,
With no mum and no dad and no home.
They are safe with me,
That I can guarantee.

I teach homeless kittens to be
patient and kind,
Until their own forever homes
we can find.
I've made it my job, do you see?
I'm really good at it, wouldn't you agree?

I snuggle and cuddle them close to my heart,
That way I know
they'll have a good start.

My kittens will find their purpose too,
And one day they'll know what to do.

While they're with me, I give them my best.
It's up to others to do all the rest.

You can help too!
We need heroes like YOU.

Buster is my name
And I won't complain.
Although I was dumped long ago,
Many people now love me, I know.

I'm so thankful for my safe, comfy spot,
It's more than many other cats have got.

I'm no longer a victim.
I have true friends and family.
I'm the king of my own Kitty Kingdom.

A Little More About Buster

On Friday, 12th November 2021, Steph Edlin alerted me to Buster's plight by posting a photo of him in our community Facebook group, asking if anyone recognised him and whether he had a home or not. Steph had been housesitting for her parents in Miramar when Buster had turned up and gazed at her through the window. His soulful eyes tugged at her heartstrings and his bad state had evoked deep concern for his welfare.

When I saw his picture, I fell in love. I felt compelled to help him and immediately got in touch with Steph. She asked her parents' permission to set a trap on the property and was told that Buster had been hanging around for years, menacing local cats in his struggle to survive.

On the Saturday, we received permission. I dropped the trap off and gave a brief tutorial on how to set it. A piece of pork crackling did the trick! Just before midnight I received a text to tell me Buster was in the bag, and I raced off immediately to fetch him. I was ecstatic. I was bringing Buster home.

He was distressed and aggressive when we got him there, so I wasn't able handle him to get a good look until morning. I simply opened the trap and he crawled directly into the igloo I'd prepared in his enclosure, and I left him to settle for the night.

I did my rounds of the cattery at 6:30 on Sunday morning and immediately noticed a great deal of blood in Buster's cage. Despite his residual fear, I risked handling him and found the gaping wound on his side. The SPCA had no emergency appointments available, so after photographing his injuries and message-bombing as many vets as I could, I was contacted by one who said Buster should be seen urgently. By then it was after 4PM, and the only option was to wait for the emergency vet to open.

and timid, but not overly aggressive. I spent hours and hours just sitting with and talking to him until, eventually, he allowed me to pat him. Once the trust was built, Buster felt comfortable sitting on me and giving as much love as he was receiving!

I raced Buster up to Ngauranga Gorge for treatment, where he was sedated and admitted straight away. I got a phone call after midnight letting me know that surgery to clean up the wound and simultaneous neutering had been successful, and that he was in recovery. The bad news was that he had tested positive for FIV, and they wanted to know if I wished for him to be put to sleep. They also said that if he hadn't received treatment when he did, he wouldn't have survived.

The decision was easy. I brought Buster home to recover. I wanted to get to know him and behaviour-test him. Buster had the cat room all to himself at that time, so I released him from his enclosure after 48 hours and let him roam free. He was scared

Buster got used to his own space and having the entire cat room to himself, but I took in three wild kittens a week later. As I sat down to check them over, Buster made a high-pitched sound which the kittens seemed to respond to. Mindful that he was FIV-positive, I tried to keep him away from the vulnerable kittens as I had no idea what he might do to them. I have seen first-hand what damage Toms can do to other cats, and to kittens especially.

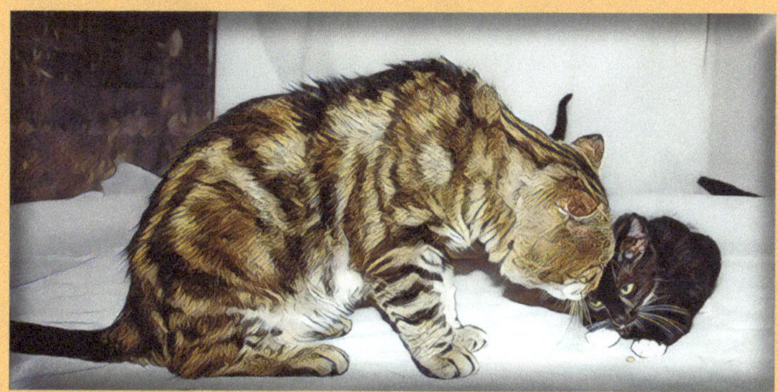

Buster seemed worried and frustrated by my not allowing him to be involved. I hesitated at first, but then reluctantly allowed him to sniff one of the kittens. The kitten sniffed him back. There was no hint of animosity from Buster: it was as if he knew the little one needed his help. He started grooming the wee kitten whose wariness immediately turned into loving purrs.

Buster went on to groom the other two while I closely monitored. It seemed the more he interacted with them, the more he NEEDED to be involved. We progressed from five minutes a day to ten minutes, then half an hour, an hour, then two hours and more, soon reaching the point of Buster telling me off if I took the kittens away from him. He pawed at my ankles or smacked my hands if I dared to remove his precious babies. In the end, I trusted the process and allowed Buster to foster them full-time. He so clearly needed to.

Buster had an appointment to sort out his rotten, broken incisors, and the surgery went well. Removing his painful teeth also lowered his chances of biting the kittens by accident, even though he's never tried to.

Just before Christmas, Buster was diagnosed with a tumour in his mouth. After three consultations, it was decided that the growth should be biopsied and removed. On the day of the operation, bloodwork was done. The results were not good: he was in the final stages of renal failure. As it was too risky to proceed, we decided to bring him home. We were concerned that the tumour would continue to grow, potentially putting the babies he loves at risk of contracting FIV should it burst or bleed. So, much to his distress, we allowed him only limited, supervised access to his babies.

We've kept Buster on as a Sanctuary Cat so that he can continue his miraculous work with kittens. He loves his job, but we do also need to monitor his health and wellbeing. He did spend a few days with another FIV-positive cat in a trial adoption, but it didn't work out and Buster came home. We are in the process of having an apartment built so that he can safely live out the rest of his life as the King of the Kitty Kingdom!

Buster has taught us much about resilience, love, compassion and kindness. Never judge a cat by its looks! Buster was born to be a grandpa, and he does a phenomenal job of it.

A few months later, I became alarmed when I saw Buster chewing on a cat bed. I expected to find that the tumour had grown or ruptured, but when I looked in his mouth, it had done neither. It had shrunk to a size the vet said was no longer of any concern! It was one of the BEST days of Buster's life when we cleared him to care for his kittens again, now with a much-reduced risk of inadvertentlyfecting them with his incurable disease.